A JOURNEY OF LOVE

through 100 Poems

Anonymous

ISBN 978-0-9883737-2-3

Published by RandomNPC LLC
Potentially Useful Information for Your Many Adventures
www.randomnpc.com

CONTENTS

Excitement

Lovers 53

As Much as Possible Love
My Cartographee
First Blush of the Morning
Unexpected Discovery
Anatomy of a Pleasant Disaster
Humble Power
Human Fusion
Propitious Obsession
A Time of Opportunity
Calm Before the Storm
Beyond Anticipation
Trip to Phantasm Light Tastik!
Admittedly
Proactive
No Asylum for You
Love is also Art Come Alive
Refuge in a Kiss
The Other Rumor of Love
Lovers Unlike the Others
Simultaneity

Closeness

Awareness

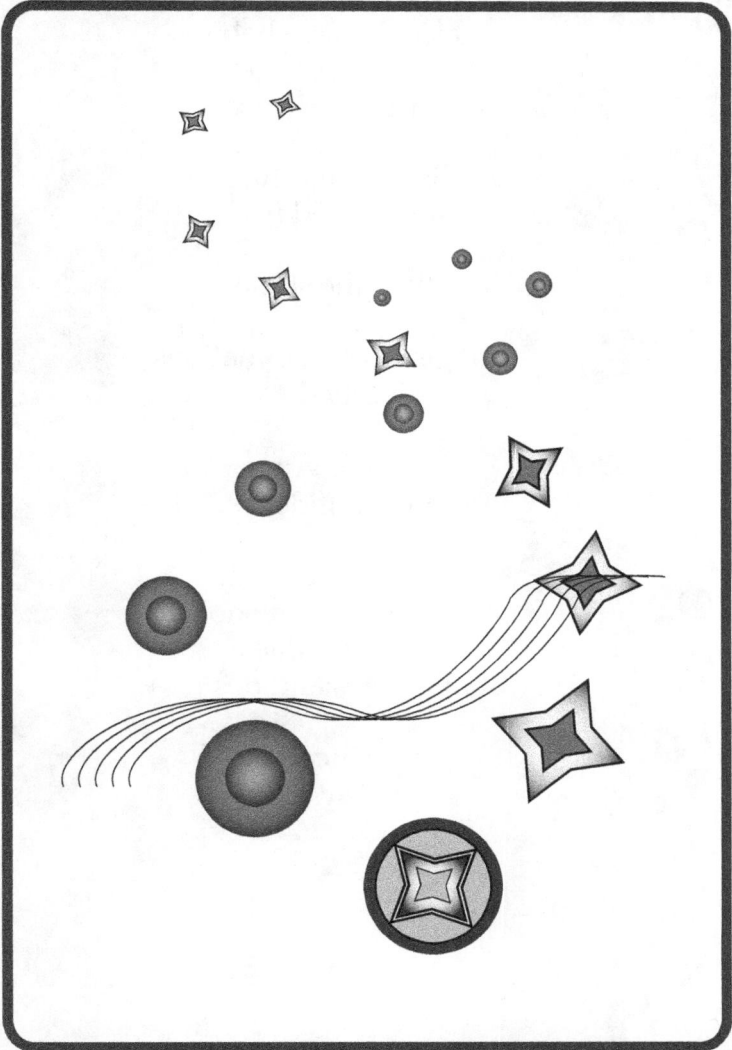

Your Transformation

First in my dreams
as the unreachable
ethereal angel
without a voice-

just a fluid turn
and a tilted head;

then the starlet
of recurring nightly
imaginatory ruminations
on a strobe-lit stage-

full of grace
and confidence;

Finally, the model
emerges from the nooks
and crannies
of my hopes and desires-

fully incarnate
in my life.

Sometimes...

it's the strangest thing:

the sun glares bronze
on the ocean in a thick
goopy gloss, and I think

that we could scrape
some off onto our toast
one morning breakfast--

instead of strawberry jam
or apple compote or grape
jelly, or even just butter.

How would it taste?

To nibble toasted bread
with sun spread thick
from crust to crust, and

maybe even dipped, piece
by shred, just a dab into
a steaming cup of java,

fed to you slowly
as you wait patiently
for the delicacy,

a morsel of morning.

Breaking the Silence

In one irresistible compliment
I forfeit my defense of
poseur cool:

Your unpretentious fresh
overpowers my yearning
and lust for freedom!

Oh, ummm, uh, ahhh,

unabashedly pure;
composed, yet exciting;
tranquil, but powerful;

so utterly
undefinable.

I am rendered unprotected
and secretly hope to become
the object of your whims.

I am now the vulnerable,
at the mercy.

Consumed

As I wake from dreams
of you I am playfully distracted
from beginning my day.

In the shower I shampoo my hair
twice as I think of you
still slumbering peacefully;

I burn my breakfast toast as I
imagine you disrobing to
enter your own shower;

while dressing I put on shoes
without any socks as I visualize
you sipping your coffee;

after buying a newspaper
I forget to take it as I picture
you fastening your earrings;

walking to the office, I circle
the same building again as the
brisk morning reminds me
of your enticing fragrance;

All day long I bluster,
happy that I am full of you
deep in my heart.

Morning Coffee

At breakfast my
thoughts of you spill

into my coffee and
I absentmindedly stir
you into the brew.

It is too late,
once I realize what
I have done,

and I discover that

coffee is much tastier
when it is
naturally sweetened.

Now I begin
every day with you
on my mind,

and the taste of
a substance sweeter
than honey
hot on my lips.

Unexpected, but Predictable

During a quiet moment
one unpredictable afternoon

we both realize that
there may be more
to the future
than

the simple sum
of its past
and present parts;

what seems to be

a destination

always turns out to be
a fresh new start,

a lull that has
already gained
momentum.

Resolve to Love

I never want to have
to think or say that

I mighta had the
courage to Coulda,

or it's possible that
I'da had the
will to Woulda,

and in retrospect
I very simply Shoulda;

when it comes to love
I wanna leap with faith

and not worry whether

I'll land safely
with my feet firmly
on the ground;

I'll just do it.

Just a Touch, but....

We touch fingertips
and it seems that we
become encapsulated
in our own insulated
private world.

The breezes cease,
the crowd's vague chattering
suddenly quiets,
my drink is numb in
my mouth,
and the fresh smell of
spring itself is neutralized.

Reality is a far-off land,

a book sitting
on my end table at home,
a video still sitting on top
of the entertainment center,
unopened letters piled askew
on the coffee table.

For our purposes,
the outside world may
as well not exist at all.

For when our fingertips touch,
I am mesmerized and struck.

Only One First Kiss

Snowballing events will soon
clamor for a decision.

Should I brush back your hair
and press my lips to your forehead?

Perhaps a quiet hint of a kiss near
your ear so that I might also
whisper a private utterance?

Or a trail of barely felt
sensations, like a delicate necklace,
laid across your throat?

Or perhaps I should adorn your arms
from your hands to your shoulders?

Would a more daring and risky
expression of passion
in a less public area be too bold?

Or a magical instant where
our lips barely touch,
in a moment of anticipation,

where the very first display of affection
is one of mutual unhurried sharing?

Our eyes are closed,
to fully savor the discovery.

Not the Heat; It's the Humidity

On a day so dark and
dismal that birds virtually
swim through the sky,

more than a couple gigs of
perfect answers lurk and look
for love's elusive questions:

the who and what, the
when, where and the why.

Sweating out predictions
of the foregone conclusions
of 20/20 hindsight,

we sheepishly await
each other's reaction to
the mystery of love's outcome,

and squeegee fingers
down the outside of tall full
soda-on-ice glasses
collecting air in beads
of condensation, so

refreshingly erudite.

Think of You

On a very odd
lack of time management
kind of day

I find myself over
an entire hour early
to some place.

What to do?

Unplanned freedom
stuns me into confusion--

what to do?

Then a simple rhyme
captures me immediately:

"What to do,
but think of you."

So as I'm pressed to do
something important
with the newfound time--

(what to do?)

I think of you!

The Desire of Rain

You are all the colors
of the rainbow speckled
into the painted landscape
of a French impressionist
in the process of discovering
the beauty of a woman
exposed in nature;

I yearn to be the rain
that nourishes the flowers
that are the speckles
in that most famous painting,

recognized by all as a
breath of fresh air
captured on canvas.

I long to be the rain
that washes away the dust;

I long to be the droplets
resting serene on your petals.

Impromptu Love Song

She's traipsed through my heart
and is now who I'm living for,
but where could she be?
¿Dónde está el amor?

She's spoken so quietly
in love's whisper, evermore;
one time I heard her vow,
"Con el cariño mi amor."

In my search for life's meaning
"break the silence!" I implore;
why won't she reveal herself?
¿Dónde está mi amor?

On the moon's cold white heart
I ceaselessly wage war;
hoping some day to find her,
¿Dónde está el amor?

Appreciated Crime

Your misrepresentation
to the world at large,

perhaps even the
perpetration of fraud,

a matter of criminal, even
more than civil, intent,

much more than an
error or omission,

of greater import than
an insurance issue,

is a brilliant façade
of naïve and demure

that is wholly untrue
when we are alone.

And your only defense
is a sheepish smile.

But I beg for you
to never atone.

Ocean Pure Blue

Your eyes tell
the story of the universe.

They display the infinite strength
of heightened awareness,
yet invite a guest to conversation.

They provoke a challenge,
yet allow for human vulnerability.

They assert the nobility of life,
and promise a tender love.

Your eyes showcase the irony
and potential of human nature,
and define a sense of paradox.

They are a glimpse of snow
drifting, and sunshine smiling.

They tell a story of intense
passion, will and insight.

Your eyes are history's
wisest storyteller.

Near Confession

I lie in bed
tossing and turning,
trying to tell the truth
as I tell you
that I want you
when that is a mere
understatement of
the fact that
the way it really is,

that I need you,
that I must have you,

just to survive
everything else.

Just the Way It Is

Laws of Nature aren't
universally applicable.

Otherwise you would know
how I feel; you would have
even just an inkling,

the proof of even just a
single iota (whatever that is)
of exactly the emotion
alive inside of me for you,
because of you.

Why doesn't osmosis work
when it comes to love?

Why can't Nature work
at just the right times, or
in the way, we want it to?

The Laws of Nature work,
apparently, only sometimes,

but not always
when we're depending
upon them

There's Always Tomorrow

Like clouds in the sky
that I can see and
try to reach, yet not feel;

to know you're there
kinda somewhere still awake,
but out of touch.

I lay awake and toss
and turn knowing you
are right there;

but I cannot call-

I don't know what it
is that you are thinking.

Now you're asleep
drifting up into clouds,
pure and white,

chaste in thought.

Rare Gem

I hold you up
to the full spectrum
sunlight of day
as you sparkle and glisten;

your spirit has
the clarity of a diamond
with perfect proportions--
it is an invisible mystery
that diffracts the
indescribable into sensations.

You translate the
underlying vibrancies of
physics into

a welcoming kiss and
long-sought embrace,

a lingering moment that
glows all night,

a memory that
reverberates without fade.

You are a gem
whose diffractive fire
blinds the world.

Our Potential

We walk to the end
of the earth and watch the sun
go down for the day;

water pours off the edge
of the planet and disappears
into infinite space.

Having found the limits
of the physical world,
we return home,
through the darkening dusk,
hand in hand,

to peer inward,
to find and discover

the rest of the world
latent in each other.

Excitement

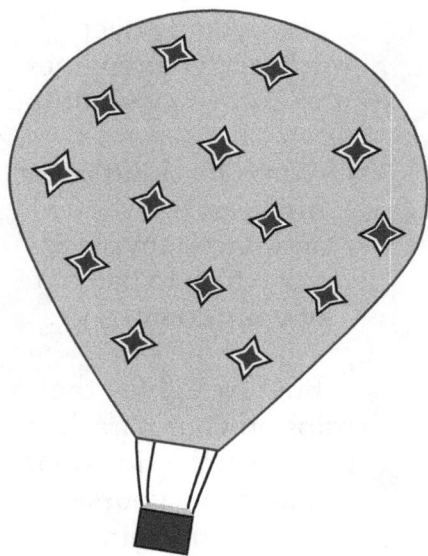

S.O.S.

The red danger light
flashes brightly!

As you fly over
my heart, your engines
sputter and you lose altitude;

obscured by cloud cover,
my heart is a vague
and uncertain place
over which to bail out
of your doomed jet.

But you tighten the
straps on your parachute,
kick open the side door,
and throw yourself
into thin air.

Seconds later you drop
from the clouds
and pull the rip cord;
after floating slowly

you then gently plop
onto my waiting heart,

safe on an emotional cushion
positioned to catch only you.

My Adventure

In your eyes
I cruise an open expanse
of clear blue ocean,

balanced between
the gravity of the sky
and the turbulence of
breezes flowing upward
from the sea;

thinking at supersonic
speeds that approach
nothing but pure emotion,

I am refreshed
by the wonder of
a fuzzied horizon,

and completely forget
even where I am.

Optimism and Kindness

My heart bursts
and vaporizes;

emotional fallout circles
the earth as my heart dilutes
into the atmosphere.

It becomes a prisoner
of Mother Nature and
swirls disoriented
around the earth,
helpless and dizzy.

Somehow you gather it
in and recover it
from the perils of
the merciless climate;

you return it to me
in a gentle kiss, or hug,
or patient caress,

ultimately
intact and safe.

Bright Moon Sky

All around us
the world is manic
with motion;

leaves are chased
by the wind,
clouds tumble
across the sky,
black night whines
through trees,
ocean surf foams,
and dust pounds
against cars.

But amidst all
this confusion
is one safe place,
a single quiet
moment of peace;

My ears are numb
to the rest
of the world
as I listen
to you speak.

Morning Promise

The esoteric ambiguity
of my thought dissipates
and I am drunk

in the mere bouquet
wafted my way

from an after-rain morning
swirled in a monster snifter
half-full of sunshine,

then poured over
your bare shoulder,

into shot glasses
you hold steady while
propped up
on a single elbow.

Tongue-Tied

You have created an
art born of exploration
and perfected
through discovery and
confession:

the admission that
there's nothing like it

anywhere
any time

any, how
maybe, "and" how.

Or something.

Anyway. Umm,
well;

Yeah….

Sweet Love for All

As I passively watch
butterflies flutter
around me in random
celebration of the sky,

I smugly think that
I am the unmoving
and stable presence
on a day giddy and
breathless with Spring;

I soon realize that
my head spins
with thoughts of you,

and the wide fresh sky
is the only temperate
sensibility not stunned

by the euphoria of
the season upon us.

Faith in Love's Storm

Helpless, I am hammered
in the downpour
of your love-

begun as a drizzle,
tempestuing from sprinkle
into full rain.

But I throw back
my head and let the
drops of refreshment
stream down my face.

It cools me
and cleanses me

and washes away
the impurities
that cause my
distress.

Miniscule in your
storm, I relent and
bathe in the
consecration.

Even Love's Poor Attempt

The extrapolation
of a smattering of symbols

where words can
only purport to describe
who you are and
what you mean to me;

for instance, when
we read a story and
imagine a character-

what she looks like,
and the sound of her voice,

or the expressions on
her face;

in the same sketchy way,
words can only do their best
in a flowery show of
good intentions,

to portray you at love's
guess, in its glamour and
rose-cheeked personage.

Momentary Distraction

You're the purple swirl
of emotion in my head,

that takes me
to places far away
from my fingers busily
tapping calculator keys
for a customer;

you're the ice cream
brain freeze that saves me
from pulsating shock waves
of heat on a summer day;

you're the final
solution to my life
outside the nine dots,
the payoff to the
practicalities;

where discovery is still
possible, and exploration
an exciting priority;

you're the ultimate dream
of a truth that brings me
through all of the illusion
and back to myself;

you're the realization
of a beautiful world
that I'd often sought,
yet only just found.

Resuscitated

In the midst of the world
I lull into cardiac arrest;
my body temperature drops and
I verge on hypothermia-

wrap me in the blanket
of your love, and
kick-start my heart
with a show of affection!

I need a sudden jolt
of passion-a surge of energy
to blast me from stillness,
to rejuvenate me back from
the numb of passive bystander.

Glob the gel on the contacts:

"Clear!" zaP/twitch,
"Again…" zAP/spasm,
"Once more…" ZAP/jerk…

beep beep…
beep beep…
beep beep…

My heart beats, I suck in breath
and continue to breathe:

My eyelids flutter,
and open; I see you
and feel you;

Once again, miraculously, I'm back
in the arms of the living.

Reassurance

I am disoriented
when I awaken
in your arms

after dreaming
about you;

Confused, I listen
to your breathing;

then I trace my finger
gently down your spine,
finally laying my open palm
flat against the small
of your back.

You reach out and
pull my lips to yours,
then settle back
into your pillow;

then I, too, melt
back into my dream.

Fruits of Our Optimism

The truth ends up
a mystical irony:

I open up to you,
and feel more protected;

I dissipate into you,
and feel more connected;

I lose myself and
discover my identity;

vulnerable to you,
I'm a stronger entity;

preoccupied by you,
my thoughts are clear;

tight in your embrace,
I'm now much freer.

Reality is now what
was unexpected.

Expression of You

As the chilly ocean breeze blows
my hair off my forehead, I smile,
then begin to whistle, as if suddenly
inspired by some good fortune;

I drink up the fresh exhalation of
the beach blowing inland, then
continue my whistling.

There is no melody--
just a long, clear note that
blends into the wind--
an unraveling of sound that
twists into tumbling air.

I create a pure sound that
augments the natural beauty
of a perfect moment--

a rush of freedom as
I think of you;

I walk on, and hold that note
impeccably, for as long as I can,
because it is the kind of wonder
that I want to create

for ever.

Oh, What Am I Saying?

You make me so silly dizzy
as if I'm being run in the sun
ragged on a hectic over-reactive day
when I'm really really bizzy!

Then I'm become just a bee buzzin,
looping around fragranty fields
full of colors, totally fully lost as if
looking for a misplaced cuzzin.

This afternoon fresh is really crazy
as I spin and, slipping, topple
beginning to feel like hopping, thinking
that dessert topping is a daisy.

You give me a PepsiCoke rush,
with adrenaline white max pumping as
I lick melting ice cream dripping down
a cone in summer brain mush.

Northbound Afternoon

Straight ahead on I-5,
I balance a world that
teeters and totters.

The huge blue ocean
on my left sprawls lazily,
inertly, as a counterweight

to the thick marshmallow
thunderheads globbed
in huge wooden spoonfuls
to the east.

The freeway is a reflective
balancing point for these two
massive contemplative forces--

the sea is more deeply
entrenched, the far off clouds
have more leverage.

I drive along, thinking of
you and me, two lovers
within a drama of
immense natural forces;

I hope that the road
doesn't suddenly tip to
one side or the other,
thrown out of kilter.

But I'm ready to swerve
in either direction

to keep my equilibrium;
I think of you.

Altered Journey of Love

As we learn about each other
we discover an unexpected.

We start out on a perimeter
and begin toward the center,
seeking the midpoint of all
the radii of a single circle's
formulaic shape.

But soon our quest
into the depths of a human
takes us no closer to our centers;

rather, we suddenly are lost
in uncharted territory,
and all points of reference
blur into ambiguity.

A lover is hardly ever,
or even never, the semblance
of any geometric shape.

But our surprises are pleasant:
A smile here. Relief there.
Excitement, hope, desire,
a yearning to meander through
the fields of butterflies that

we both feel. Passion
compels us to explore,

and it seems that
there is no turning back
from undefined reality.

We traipse through our hearts,
content to have no destination.

Love's 911

I am sorry
for the blood
on your hands;

but I appreciate
your first aid:

when my heart
becomes a pincushion
for every warrior's
sword as he
attacks to practice,

as he earns a point
towards success,

you extract the
weapon, clean the
wound, and apply
healing salve.

Then I help you
wash the stain
from your hands.

The least
that I could do.

Call the Road Side Service of Love

Like a sightseer
fishtailing out of control
on an unfamiliar winding
coastal road,

on a Sunday drive
there for the taking,

having taken his eyes
off the curves for
a split second to
glance out over
the ocean,

and now caught
in a moment of
unplanned anxiety,

my love for you
has lost its sense
of control and
self-confidence

as it yanks the
steering wheel back and
forth, overcorrecting,

careening one side
to and fro the other.

Decision to Love

The world is avoid;
I seek only you.

I shun the crowded highways,
and glide along the byways
lost in pleasant preoccupation.

Nothing distracts my attention
as you fill my mind with
remembrances, and promises
of futures even better
than our memories.

I elude the now lonely seclusion
of sweet solitude, cashed in
for sharing any amount
of time with you.

From the world I refrain,
to sing a song with you.

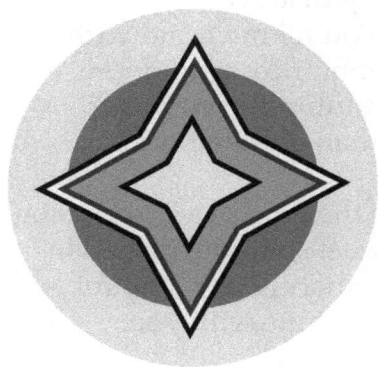

Lovers

As Much as Possible Love

I think about making
love to you
only

when I'm awake;

I dream about making
love to you
only

when I'm asleep;

I'm all about making
love to you
only

every time I can,

which, luckily,
is more often

than most others
consider the times

it takes to
define,
"getting lucky."

My Cartographee

You are so much fun
just lounging face down
in bed, letting me play
connect-the-dots,

numbered only in my mind,

following the freckles
on your back;

before long I have drawn
a complete map
of our destinations
by gently dragging
my fingernail
across your skin.

Then you let me chart
a course and navigate
into uncharted territory,

like a Christopher Columbus
bankrolled by a secretly
satisfied Queen,

and I sail toward the edge
of the world, beyond the map,
into the great Unexplored,

where only lovers go,
and only love
can be trusted to survive.

First Blush of the Morning

Morning light streams in
to our bedroom, adding nature's heat
to the coziness of our love.

We throw off the covers
and lay out across the sheets bare
in our unshy comfort with each other;

I place one last kiss on you,
like a butterfly artfully
lighting on a violet bloom;

well, you deserve more than just
a single conclusive caress--

perhaps a delicate bouquet of kisses,
as that which a butterfly could collect,
if it were much larger, while unhurriedly
exploring a field rich with wildflowers.

After some time we
throw our feet over the edge of the bed,
and stand to accept the invitation
of a brand new sun:

we twist and turn to stretch,
and extend our arms upward
toward the rays of light,

exhaling our last yawns
as our farewell to the dawn.

A Journey of Love

Unexpected Discovery

When we make love
I become the universe,

a sense of euphoria
that supports the graceful
gliding of birds free in the sky,

a timelessness that
engulfs space,
infinite mass that
absorbs time.

I become the essence of
a floral fragrance,

the original insight of
a great thinker,

the perfect answer
to a child's pondering.

Yet, most importantly,
as we share the intensity,
as we open ourselves
to each other,

and hold each other
with our eyes wide open,

I finally feel that I am
in sync with myself,

by sharing myself with you,

and I sense that I finally
understand the goodness
of the universe.

Anatomy of a Pleasant Disaster

Inside the nuclear reactor
of life, you escalate
a stable situation of love
into the meltdown crisis
of uncontrollable lust;

yanked out the control rods!

monitor the temperature-

it climbs into the red zone;
the needle taps frantically
against the maximum!

Energy saturates physical
space and the kinetic
overload becomes unbearable;

the intensity of the
chain reaction passes
instrumentation limits

into a no-man's land
of passion that
only a fearless heart
can fathom.

Humble Power

The entire world
is subdued by darkness
as you sleep.

It is comatose as
you slumber;
the world has no purpose
while it waits.

The world is forced
to be patient,
but it pouts
in sullen discontent.

Finally you awaken,
and stretch, and rise
into a brand new day;

the sun hustles up
over the horizon
to greet you and

the world is given silent
permission
to begin again, and

it endeavors to
pay you homage for
bringing it to life.

Human Fusion

For rampant weeks
when I think of you

all I know

is how I feel endless
as a universe of stars
explodes inside of you.

With destiny expanding
at an increasing rate,

I surge with
incalculable power--

our love encompasses
points of reference,
overlapping timeframes and
historical contexts.

We enact all of this
most effortlessly,

most gracefully,

in a supernova of
internal sunlight.

Propitious Obsession

To make you feel
so good that
you lose yourself

and become unconscious

of anything but
the sensation-

it engulfs you;

you dissolve in it.

The feeling becomes
your awareness

and time hovers,
becomes weightless,

like a gasp
of pleasure
so subtle

that it snacks by
gingerly nibbling

on the ragged
edges of
fluffy clouds.

A Time of Opportunity

Evening fog blows in
as commuters jam
the freeways home.

As if the city were
a birdcage suddenly
covered by a blanket,
the fog blocks out the
scattered sunset.

Animals settle and
nestle into their burrows
as only stray sparrows
flit from tree to tree--

an activity resembling
more an afterthought
than a resolution.

We close the blinds,
turn out the lights,

and retreat under covers
to snuggle and share

in complete surrender
to a rare and lazy evening
lost to fingertips
and tongues.

Calm Before the Storm

My face buried
in a silky splash
of scented hair

close to you,
coming to my senses
after dreaming,

I dare not move
even a single muscle
for fear that you

might wake and
stretch and yawn
alive from slumber

and prematurely
welcome the new day
that would beckon.

Beyond Anticipation

We compose intimate
verbal exchanges
that lead to…

We invent indescribable
nonverbal interludes
the end up…

We lose control
of our
communication

on a whim
on evening blustery outside
on not even a dare
on a bear rug inside

right in front of a
blazing fire.

Trip to Phantasm Light Tastik!

is an unique phenomenon
we can nickname
the Northern Lights of Dream,

caught in the whoosh of time
in a deep slumber, restfully

amazed and dazed by explosions
of light subdued by doting on you--

the object of fantastic desire;

a good night's steep of fresh tea

steaming in a ceramic cup cradled
in my mind's eye hands, warmth

keeping my fingergrasp clinging
curled around its glossy curvature

in a retro repose as
I remember the numbing dazzle
of the night before.

Admittedly

They say that
to be human,
a human needs
to be touched;

I don't know
the statistics,
but I do know
that I do.

And I love
the time of day
when you say
that you know, too;

you say that
I will touch you
in ambiguous
unlimited ways.

A Journey of Love

Proactive

Like climbing up
slippery shale
subsisting on the
passionate exhale

of sheer desire;

peace in the repose
of the aftermath of
expended energy;

in-between heartbeats

relaxing in the resting
of the counterpoint;

we take our love
into the dangerous world
with a vengeance
against all odds.

No Asylum for You

Having incinerated every
cloud from the sky,

the sun bears down
with insinuated scorn
in its intensity;

but it is just being
itself, appearing so simple
in the sky-far distance,
so yellow and soft.

It harbors no disdain,
yet its heart is
a complexity of thrashing
hydrogen fusion explosions,
flurries of dense
and invulnerable emotions,

not unlike the passion
that swells within me

as my eyes dote on you,
as you walk
all the way from the tub,

and as you pause
and your toes drip water
onto the bath mat,

to your robe hanging
in the closet.

Love is also Art Come Alive

At the art exhibit I tire of inspecting
nudes of fat women from the past

and begin to watch you
respectfully admiring
portraits of dead women painted by dead artists;

after bestowing your appreciation on one
16th, 17th, 18th or whatever long-gone
century's substitute for photography,

you pause to use the glass over the painting
as a mirror to check your make-up and
brush stray hairs away from your forehead.

--enough sedentary drivel !!!!!
I should take you to the stairwell
and pay you my own homage-

I would recognize THE true artistic genius still
relevant in all respects that truly matter:
I would give God his due for creating you;

to smear your perfect lipstick
with a gusto kiss I would instantly capture
the intent of the gallery;

not waiting for compliments from gawkers;
I would transform beauty into a performing art
and, thus, validate its integrity.

Refuge in a Kiss

Your kiss brings closure
to a thousand antic
ramblings, fears of thought
and trepidation in the
face of objective reality;

thinking creates technology
that keeps butter hard;

feeling is the heat that
rounds a cube's edges,

then is responsible for
its melting into shapeless
lump and blob as it mixes
with the soup broth-

butter becomes the flavor
that I taste on your lips
after our bellies are full

from dinner, and we have
shut down technology
all around the house

and we've retired from
the thinking and the strife
of the workday.

The Other Rumor of Love

Whispers and caresses
are unproven suspicions
in the interim unknown between
nightfall and morning;

the mere chat and blab
of circumstantial evidence falls
unconvincingly short in the absence
of the night's only witness.

And, ultimately, the mirthful
white moon has but a
mere fleeting memory
in its romance of the earth,

and cares nothing about
the victimless crimes of
lovers now lost
in love's joyous birth.

Lovers Unlike the Others

They say that
they are condemned
to life by
the laws of Nature;

we do not understand
them because we know

that our spirits need
a carnal essence
to appreciate each other
in our private
meeting of the minds.

Our bodies live out
the fantasies of
our imaginations;

our bodies commit
the very sins of
our intentions.

Simultaneity

When the lighted match
of your body falls

onto the spilled gasoline
of my very soul,

we ignite in combustive
ecstasy, and I hold you
as close as possible

so that we may evaporate

from reality to euphoria
at the very same instant.

Closeness

Hope Becomes Real

We channel the
sometimes excruciating pain
of consciousness,

and translate
the yuck and the muck
of sensations we feel

(alienation,
disorientation,
desperation)

into the passion
of a delicate touch

shared with each other
in a bond of trust
that transcends

all fear,
all sense of risk,
all vulnerability,
all doubt;

it seems that
we double the love
that exists
in the universe

by loving each other.

We Just Understand

Our lonely pasts intersect
in a lush green meadow;

we offer each other a drink
from our canteens, but
finally just dump out the
stale liquid and refill them
with fresh running spring water.

We listen to the birds noisy
in the thickets, the stream
patient in its search for the sea,
the trees caressed by the breeze;

we languish in the afternoon sun--
Nature fills us with warmth
and gives us time to learn about
each other without distractions.

In our discussion we develop
a new appreciation for the
beauty of the world.

Our friendship enhances
what we'd already felt,
while fortifying what we
thought we'd known.

The Messenger Moon

You are somewhere far away,
on the other side of the country,
on the opposite side of
a satellite's relayed signals.

I tell the moon what I think
and ask it to deliver my message;
surely I can trust it to translate

without any loss of meaning
in rephrasing feeling to thought,

without misrepresenting my
intentions because of laziness,

without forgetting even some
slight detail of my colloquy.

On a clear cold night, when the
moon is full, and there are no clouds
to distract it, I only hope that
it gives you my thoughts completely.

I only wish for you to feel
what I feel, as I speak to it, as I
ask it to deliver my sentiments.

I assume that if you can't trust
the moon, then who can you rely upon?
To pass on a simple message
from my heart, anyway;

so, now, please take a moment
to lift your eyes to the moon,
to pause, and to listen.

One of Those Days

On one of those
articulate days when

we talk our hearts out,
but never really feel
that we've said anything,

I quietly approach you,
take your hands in mine,
confiscate your pen,

and lay your fingers
upon my face.

Then I kiss your palms,
and your fingertips, one by one,

because I appreciate
how communicative they can
be without words.

For a long unspoken moment
we share an understanding

about an intangible something
people spend lifetimes
of sentences
trying to quantify,

then merely end up having
spewed a bunch of
words and punctuation

that just got
lost in the translation.

Evening Walk

We saunter along
the sidewalk
through the drizzle,

surprised by a heavy mist
suddenly thick enough
to sag like wet paint
dripping down a
freshly brushed wall;

our initial reaction is
to hurry our pace, but soon
we slow up enough to drink
in the dissolving sky,

rather than flee from it,
which is impossible, anyway!

We clasp hands and
continue toward home,
our exchanged body heat
sufficient to ward off
any kind of damp chill.

Together we enjoy
the refreshment of rain
as it disintegrates
the endless sky.

A Journey of Love

Spring Love: The Miracle

Sometimes you never know,
so we plant the bougainvillea
and just go about our business;

after a few weeks
we suddenly realize that
it is full of fresh growth
and its tendrils are desperately
reaching out in search
of support;

we scramble to erect
a good-sized trellis
behind it, then pour a
solution of B12 around
its roots, amazed

and pleasantly surprised.

We are finally encouraged
by our green thumbs
as we stand under the
sunshine in our garden,

hoping that the vine grows
beyond the sky.

Negotiating a Lover's Truce

I uncross your arms,

then spend a long time
gently inspecting the shape
and texture and delicacy
of your hands,

and trace their outlines
very slowly and quietly,
so as to not miss any
subtle curve or softness.

Finally, after quite a while,
I intertwine my fingers
with yours and contentedly

revel in the peacefulness
of the moment, for as
long as it lasts.

My Friend, the Sun

Bathed by sunlight
your face is a subtle
memory of experience,

a hint of evolution

from pain to kindness,
from doubt to trust,

a chronicle of joy, reflection,
and ultimate forgiveness
of the world's senselessness.

Then your smile tells me
that you have the courage
to embrace the future,

that you are an
indestructible optimist
who grows forward.

The sun brings me your
innermost secrets,
which I am honored
to protect.

The sun, it turns out,
exists only to help me
appreciate you.

The Power of Silence

You forgive me for being
hopelessly inarticulate, and
carry the conversation upwards
like a skilled mountain climber
scaling Mount Everest.

I fumble for words and mumble
to keep you from hearing the
jumble of sounds I cannot form.

One night I caress
the palm of your open hand
with exploratory kisses, and follow
its creases with my lips.

I begin to whisper the words
that can only fake the utterance of
how I feel, but you cover
my mouth with your hand

and stare into my eyes.
You tell me, "Ssshhh...."

I am relieved. You uncover my
mouth, gratefully mute, then
softly press your lips to mine

so that we may convey
truths without anything
being lost in the
translation of sentiment
into symbols.

Finally Done Right

In the
lazily basking
of our respite,

our visit becomes
a framed memory

rather than a
bluuur of quiet

sandwiched between
two contiguous
crazy moments

nearly overlapping
and distraught
with white noise.

Another Rumor of Love

Whispers and caresses
characterize the language
that defines
the literally undocumented

conversations that permeate
the interim
between night and day;

only the pure moon
and its manipulated shadows
could bear witness
to our private moments,

yet the moon is
too chaste to do more
than note the gossip
of the vapid night.

Unmixed Messages

As I pour emotions
from the pitcher
of my heart,

all the right words remain
on the bottom
like unstirred orange juice,

sort of a sweet sludge
undelivered to your glass.

Sometimes I feel
like I need a wooden spoon
to mix the substance
with the intentions,

but somehow I just
can't find it in my junk
drawer of words.

I know I have a spoon
here somewhere,
let me see--

thanks for being patient
while I rummage
around a little bit.

The normal verbiage
that I use for everyone
else will just not do.

Someone I Can Trust

When I lay down to sleep,
and become vulnerable
to unconsciousness and
the unstructured vast of night,
I want to be snug
in your arms. My drifting dreams

need a point of reference,
a frame of reference, if you will,
something less formal than
a letter of reference, yet
something with more substance,

as I hitch-hike along the
vapor trails of the universe
at the speed of imagination.

I want someone who will do more
than give me a lift to the
next portal of fateful possibility.

After I trek back
from my final sleepful destination,
I must quickly wake from the brainstorm
to experience the full reality of

the clearest dream of them all,
your snuggle and cuddle,
and protective embrace.

Love Is Its Own Reward

I suggest that
we find no reason
to extol
the spurious moment.

With no justification,
let's just do it!

Let's contradict
the repugnant phony,
and perform our
own ceremony;

we celebrate love
as an experience
rather than recognize
its subsequence

as a business format.
Against the future: Splat!

The act that defines
a relationship is
its own applause

and rite in and
of itself.

I propose that we
discover each other
once more.

Offstage, in the Audience

Downtown, at the Saturday
evening opera, in the dark, I watch
you watching and wonder, as the light
radiates in a glow off the main stage;

you turn nonchalantly and smile
innocently as I whirl inside of you
and wonder at my stage fright
as you whisper inquire, "what?"

But I can't explain the what,
the trepidation, since I never meant
to care again any more since I hadn't
even met you yet, not even you.

Onstage, emotion is the intangible
meaning of the dialogue sung by
the players, the improvisational part
of the lines they have memorized.

Unaware of this paradox
they continue to reiterate, yet create,
using their skills and abilities
to transcend a mere performance.

The actors carry on, even though
the truth is a frightening thing,
worthy of any wonder, yet lost
in potently ambiguous "ohmygod".

Just a Quick Note

To transmit a
meandering insight

gleaned from weaving
in and out of,
gyrating around,
and wobbling about,

myriad concepts

spun off of
shifting perspectives

while dwelling
upon you

instead of working;
I think of you

and am left with
only an impression

of an intangible angel
not bound by
single thoughts

but, rather,
inspired by infinite
feelings.

A Thought While Walking on the Beach

The new material
revelation is the approximate
transfiguration of energy
into pure figure
and unmistakable form;

holding your hand
is the ultimate nuance
and the understatement
of some concatenant
everlasting passion;

and, especially tonight,
that warmth is hors d'oeuvre
of a stir-fry celebration
feast yet strewn in the pan
and simmering.

Pre-emptive Mortality

Aimlessly seeking angels
pursue you,

And infinitely evil Satan
covets your time;

But under the cover
of transcendent reality

I steal you away,

Since in your incumbent
flesh and blood,

you're all mine.

Hendrixish Love Insight

After wandering aimlessly
through the sagebrush
of my mind,

I finally plop down
in the desert sand,

exhausted and disoriented,
dehydrated and parched,
hallucinating in the heat;

at last I am ready
to be consumed and,
ultimately, transformed,
from a transient
state of matter;

I am prepared
to give myself up
to my destiny:

I have only one
single-minded desire-
to be consumed
within your fire.

Protecting Love from Entropy

When it seems
that my love is
potentially infinite,

I remember placing
my flat palm on the cold
marble stone below the lion
in Trafalgar Square:

with the chill raining down
on pigeons clustered,
well, more like "huddled",

together like miniature auditors,
their chins buried in their chests
to hoard some warmth,

and I realize, again,
no, duh,

that the coldness of
the world is overwhelming,
and colder than my touch;

so I save my caress
for you, and my warmth
for the person who
really matters.

Forever

Refreshing Essence

At first
you are a waterfall

free-falling
through mountain chill
from breath-taking and
scenic heights;

then you are
the weightless mist
catching the sun
in rainbows,

drifting lightly and
settling into the
pool of snowmelt

to become the swirling
eddies of near-frozen,
just unfrozen, white,

now clear and pure
in perfect transparency.

Finally I sip you up
from a cup dipped
into your temporary
gathered tranquility-

a taste, perhaps,
of your very soul,

just before
you resume your journey
downstream.

Just in Time

I trudge through the storm;

angry winter snow screams
hysterically; I am blind inside
the turmoil of drifting frozen
air void of compassion. I am
warmthless and nearly numb.

But then I glimpse the
flames of a campfire fighting
to burn amidst the confusion.

You are there tending
the fire, feeding it new fuel,
protecting it against the wind.

I join you next to the fire
and you wrap your coat
around me, and we are warm--
together and safe.

You pull us snug inside blankets
and I begin to thaw:

I appreciate your strength and
the regenerating transcendence
of your optimism.

I am in total awe.

I Am Mistaken

Just a minute;
stop for a moment!

You are perfect
except for a tiny eyelash
fallen onto your cheek.

Pause briefly, momentarily;
there now, don't move.

I wet my fingertip
with a dab onto my tongue,
then reach towards you
to gently lift the eyelash
from your face.

No, no. No!
What does it matter?
An eyelash is nothing.

I assuage your surprise
with a sheepish smile as
I dry my fingertip, with a twist,
on my shirt.

I leave the eyelash on your cheek.
You are always perfect.

Love as a Strategy

In our unspoken pledges
we entrust each other
with vulnerabilities
that we don't even know
about ourselves;

in our labor of love
we refuel smiles with sunrise,
and acknowledge the sunsets
as they lure away the
last remaining daylight.

In our chess game
with the world we search
our hearts for survival tactics
to move successfully
against the timer;

in our lust for living
we rage, rage against
the dying of what might
really be an answer disguised
within the question.

In our own ambiguities
and uncertainties we may wonder,
but we stoke the fires of action
so that, ultimately, we will
die with our boots on.

Renewal

From the grog of
recent slumber, I shake
the drowsiness, and browse
through the anticipation
of the upcoming day;

In a brief lapse from the crash
of scattered plans, my pause
and reflection is filled by you:

you are like the rich cream
of the swirl in my coffee
that I sip to prepare for
the world,

that I drink to engage
my awareness,

you are the ingredient that
enriches the flavor of my life;

after you on my tongue
I feel the earth's strength
in the new sunshine.

The fog and the dark
soon evaporate from haze,
and birds chatter and sing.

Out of dreams I amble
into the newfound joy
of love that you bring.

My Heart's Articulation

My answers to your questions
are the promises that I make
after there's no reason
to win your love.

They are the things I say
in the denouement of passion;

it is the tenderness
after the lust,
the last kiss on your neck
under your brushed-back hair
as we rest, and catch our breath.

The answers are all
the things that I am that
I offer in my vulnerability,

the inconvenient honesty,
the imperfect reality
of my intentions,
the realization of my
attempts to make you smile;

All the answers to
your questions, I yearn
to make known,

for while they are yours,
they're also my own.

A Paradox of Priorities

We discover that neither
their bottom line, nor the big
picture, has any relevance;

it turns out that the little
things that nobody ever notices
are the shining stars in the
infinite black sky of
a personal lifetime.

Being close to a tiny star
makes it a huge sun;

whispering to you in a crowd
with my lips brushing against
your cheek and ear makes a
public place intimately personal;

saying that I love you
after I have nothing left
to give is the real difference.

Timelines are endless ideas
that become nonchalantly extended
for someone's convenience,

and our love is an
unknown and irrelevant
part of their universe.

The rampant imperfections of
a world's ambitions
become our true allies as,

together, we travel the universe.

The Rescue

Today is an avalanche
that buries me--

nearly suffocated, I crawl,
barely alive, from debris
inertly piled on me,

nearly crushing me with
its sheer weight:

rejection,
disappointment,
failure,
rudeness,
uncertainty,
fear.

Finally, at the end
of this catastrophic day,
I am with you.

Falling asleep in your arms
is the only hope I have left.

Reflective

On one of those
touch and go days
with the sun in battle
against the clouds;

I am dull to sensation,

torn apart inside
by intangible
possible futures-
the unknowable answers
to the "what if...s."

The silver haze
slowly turns to
blackening gray:

the sun must be
setting on the
unseen horizon,

and I check my
pockets for change

to call you
before it gets dark.

SoulMates as Expressionists

We make waves
in the universe:

when the world is calm
our intertwined minds amp
up the energy level
to create a ripple effect--

like a pebble, our love
splashes into the calm
of a sleeping world
and the energy radiates
in concentric circles;

and when life is crazy,
our ecstasy ameliorates
the confusion and distress
into unpredicted serenity
amidst all the racket--

the insanity of a world
tense and smitten drains
toward our love and
is magically neutralized:

We create peace
in the universe.

Like Banana Silly Love

Peeling away
mature, the mere years,

to the essence
to the energy,

you are the cute
and I become the cuddly.

Bring me inside
where nothing has changed
and you say it all

without a word
but the warmth
and the lost
inside the dream

the true reality.

A Drop of Love...

...,Just About to Drip, Hanging from
the Water Faucet of my Brain, Leaking
Because of an Old Worn Washer

You are
the personification

of a rainbow's potential
cultivated

from my imagination
into full-blossom
reality

Fortune Teller

After life-long training,
or based on some
mystical in-bred talent, they can
tell the future by reading tea leaves
in the bottom of a cup;

More importantly, though, I can predict
our future by peering into the swirls
of cream poured into the center
of a full mug of strong coffee!

I see…smiles twisting in and out
of the steaming brew as the two liquids mix;
water evaporates to become an invisible
fragrance throughout the dining room-
it leaves a more potent
flavor to partake of in the mug.

Okay, and I see…, YES! it's quite clear…
a good-morning savor lingering
on our palate-- a comfort-food aroma
alive in our nostrils--
the twinkle of merriment sparking in our eyes--

these are all the signs
that one might see
clearly in a crystal ball.

How Love Survives

The forgotten past is
a dry handful
of fire-danger fuzz
that we compact
into a loose ball
with our fingertips;

we place it under
a pile of teepee kindling,

extract a single match,
slide the match box shut,
scrape the match tip
along the side of the box…

the flame bursts alive,
flares, then relapses
into a steady burn
of anticipation.

The flame touches the fuzz
and hungrily feeds
on the dehydrated life,

reigniting itself blazing
anew, growing fervent
in its self-sufficiency.

The Tail End of Winter

We breeze up Encinitas
Blvd. gratefully using the full
moon as our North Star;

we gulp in draughts
of cool early springtime air
in an amazing place where
there really is no brutal chill
of residual winter.

The resplendent moon is
a perfect white light
without a lampshade;

it brightens our clear black
night on the coast, a most
welcome guest in a collage
of nature's expressions.

To our bursting hearts' content
we're free to explore away,
to discover nooks and crannies
in moonshine bright as day.

Your Healing Touch

Day becomes twilight, then
the darkness of endless night.

Dreams turn to dragons
that pursue me, and drive me
into mazes of chaos.

Once caught,
I am digested by demons,

first trapped, then discarded.

Disoriented, I lay stunned,
merely half-conscious,

with only hopes
without substance.

But you become the morning,
the sunshine outside,

the light that draws me to open
the shutters and let the day in.

My life could now become
meaningful again, somehow.

I want to become
myself again.

Land of Crypticopia

Still in search
of the perfect words,

I backpack through
landscapes of love,
hoping to set up camp
before nightfall;

I collect only more
sensations and nebulous
impressions-full of
wonder and mystery-
yet none of them subject
to translation.

Even in this wilderness,
rich with thrill, I must
attempt to converse, though,
for one never knows
if the campsite is
just around the
very next bend.

In lieu of the unflawed
utterance, a tent cozy
with companionship warm

in the cold night always
transcends the moment's
capture and trap
within linguistic symbols.

True Love is Undefined

Upside potential is
the unknown and
the unpredictability
of our love,

unsure of what is next
and where it will lead
and how it might
turn out

at any given point
in time.

This is the true beauty
of it all;
it is not cast in concrete.

As a dynamic process
it is a living thing,
shapeless, unclear, evolving.

Our love is not
a self-imposed life sentence,

nor an untended garden
overgrown with weeds;

nor is it something neglected
and taken for granted,

like a material object
once coveted but
now dusty and forgotten
on the top shelf.

No Dimensions

Our love is energy
without a time frame:

Describing it in terms
of a past isn't relevant as
we grow forward;

the present has the most
urgency, but cannot contain it;

the future offers the most
promise, but is still just
an understatement of
our potential.

Our love transcends
the four dimensions of
existence itself:

it has no
height, width, depth
or temporality!

Our love is the paradox
of modern physics,

having none of the
standard characteristics
used to describe things,

containing elements of
only mystery,
awe and compassion.

Suggestion of the Sea

To hear the memory
of a whisper;

to live without
knowing the secret of life
is the secret of life,
and the ultimate wisdom
that we can never know
in its clearest entirety;

to feel the wind
even when it's not blowing;

to give ourselves
to each other in a love
that we have sought
our whole lifetimes,

wondering where we have been
and if it's really true:

to accept a most
glorious fate,

and spend my life
with you.